Usborne

My First Book About

Our World

Usborne Quicklinks

To visit websites with activities and fun facts about our planet, go to www.usborne.com/quicklinks and type in the keywords "first book about our world".

Website researcher: Jacqui Clark

Contents

My First Book About
Our World

Felicity Brooks

Illustrated by Mar Ferrero

Edited by Caroline Young and
Hannah Wood

Designed by Francesca Allen
and Kirsty Tizzard

Our world

Our world is a planet called the Earth.
It's shaped like an enormous ball.
From space it looks a little like this.

The green shapes are land. It is divided up into continents.

Europe is one of Earth's continents. There are six others.

North America

Europe

The blue parts are the oceans. This is the Atlantic Ocean.

Africa

Equator

South America

Antarctica

You can't see the continents of Australia or Asia here as they're on the other side of the Earth.

The red line marks the equator round the middle of the Earth. You can't see it in real life.

Where in the world do you live?

The continents are divided up into nearly 200 countries. Do you know which one you live in?

Anna lives at 14 East Street. Her street has lots of houses on it.

East Street is one of many streets in the town of Smallton.

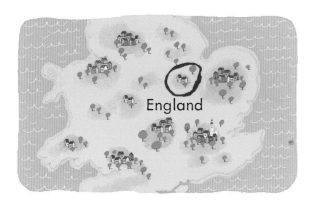

Smallton is one of many towns in Anna's country, England.

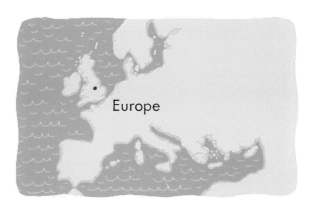

England is one of many countries in the continent of Europe.

Europe is one of the seven continents on planet Earth.

The Earth is one of eight planets in space that go around the Sun.

What's in our world?

Some things in our world were made by people, but many were not. All the things on this page are natural – they weren't made by people.

How many of these words do you know?

rainforest

volcano

grassland

forest

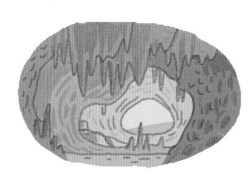

cave

desert

iceberg

mountains

seashore

All these things were made by people. They are man-made.

factories

cities

farms

ports and harbours

Which of these things do you think are natural, and which are man-made?

The answers are on page 32.

leaf

hat

book

button

cup

stone

feather

shell

The world's weather

The things that make all the world's weather happen are the Sun, air and water.

When the air around us moves very quickly in gusts, it's windy.

When the sky is clear, the Sun can shine on the Earth, so it's sunny.

If it's very cold, the water in rain freezes into snowflakes, so it's snowy.

When droplets of water in clouds join together and fall, it's rainy.

Strong wind and rain mean it's stormy. There may be lightning and thunder too.

If it's foggy, tiny droplets of water in the air make it hard to see very far.

What makes it rain?

All water on Earth comes from rain and snow, but there's never any new water. The same rain falls again and again.

This picture shows why it rains. This is called the water cycle.

cloud

Sun

3 The droplets join together and fall as rain onto the land, rivers and seas.

2 Some water turns into tiny droplets which rise up and form clouds.

1 The Sun heats the water in rivers, lakes and oceans.

lake

sea

river

4 Rivers flow back into the sea.

land

9

The seasons

The world's weather changes with the seasons. Each year has four seasons and you can see different things in each one.

Spring

Summer

In spring, plants grow and animals have babies. Birds make nests, lay eggs and look after the chicks when they hatch.

Summer is the warmest season. Trees are covered with leaves, flowers bloom and fruit ripens on bushes and trees.

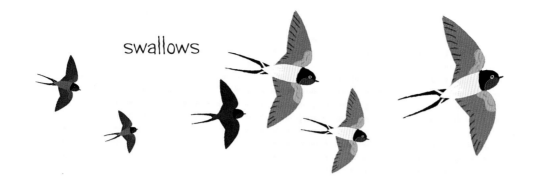

swallows

When it starts to get cold, some birds fly to warmer parts of the world. This is called migration.

Autumn

Winter

In autumn, animals get ready for winter and some hide food. Many trees lose all their leaves and plants stop growing.

Winter is the coldest season, and few things grow. Some animals sleep right through it. This is called hibernation.

The route of a river

Rivers carry water from the rain and melting snow that falls on hills and mountains down to the sea.

Try learning the things that the river passes along the way, then covering the labels and saying them aloud.

mountains

hill

When snow on the mountains melts, the water flows downhill in streams.

stream

valley

Streams may join together like these to make a river.

As the river winds its way down to the sea, it gets wider.

waterfall

Who lives here?

Rivers are home for lots of birds, fish and other animals. Can you name these animals? The answers are on page 32.

a)   b)   c)   d)   e)

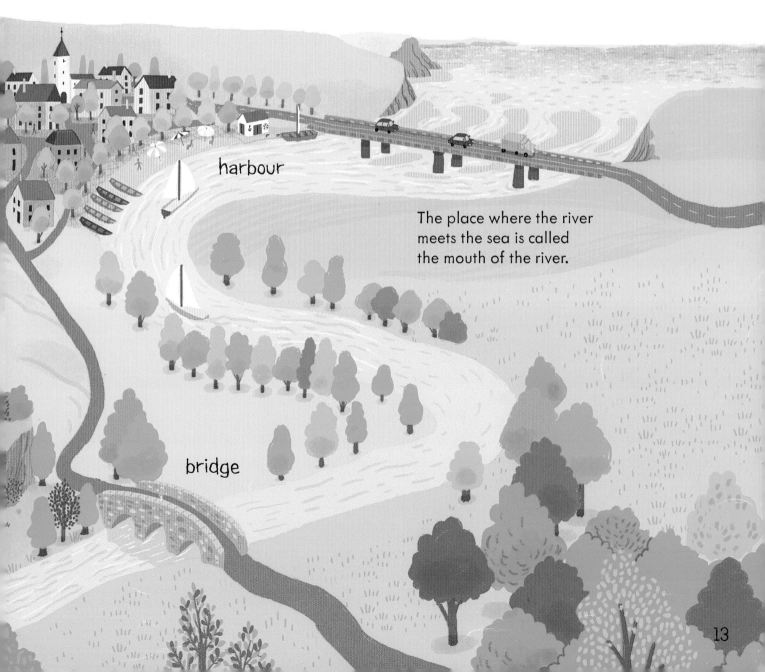

harbour

bridge

The place where the river meets the sea is called the mouth of the river.

Seas and oceans

Almost three-quarters of the Earth is covered with seas and oceans. They are full of amazing animals and plants.

seagulls

This island is the top of a mountain. Most of it is under the sea.

squid

octopus

turtle

a shoal of fish

ray

The world's oceans

There are five main oceans. Cover the labels and see if you can remember their names.

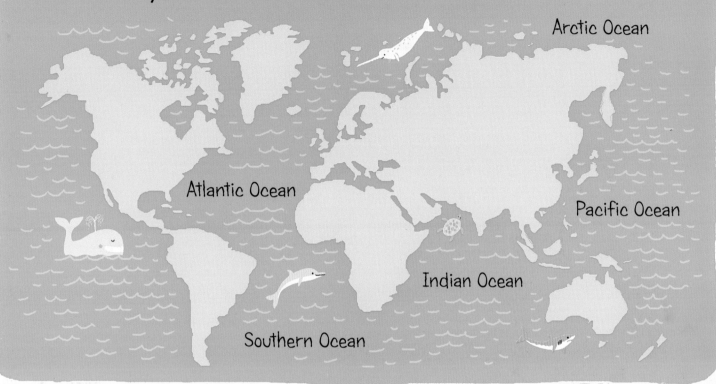

Arctic Ocean

Atlantic Ocean

Pacific Ocean

Indian Ocean

Southern Ocean

dolphin

jellyfish

shark

Coral reefs

In the warm oceans of the world, millions of tiny sea animals join together to make a coral reef, like this one.

Coral reefs are home to a huge number of fish and other animals.

Kinds of coral

These corals grow in the biggest reef in the world, near Australia. It's called The Great Barrier Reef.

The names of these corals are: bubble coral, sea fan, brain coral and bird's-nest coral. Can you guess which is which? Answers on page 32.

a)

b)

c)

d)

Divers visit reefs to see the amazing coral and fish.

Rainforests

Rainforests, or jungles, grow in the hot areas of the world around the equator. It rains almost every day in rainforests.

A few trees grow very tall. They get plenty of sunlight.

These trees grow close together and shade the forest floor.

It's easy for animals to hide in the thick trees and plants just above the ground.

Hardly any light reaches the forest floor, so it's dark and gloomy.

Where do they live?

These animals all live in different parts of the Amazon Rainforest in South America.

Birds such as macaws fly high above the tree tops and out into the sunshine.

Sloths spend their time moving very slowly in the trees above the ground.

Snakes slither around on the ground and up into the trees to catch food.

Shy animals such as this jaguar hide on the shadowy floor of the forest.

Deserts

Deserts are places where little rain falls. They can be very hot in the day and freezing at night.

This hill of sand is called a sand dune.

In parts of deserts there are strange, big craggy rocks.

An oasis is a place with water where plants can grow.

It's hard for animals to live in these hot, dry places, but here are some that do.

This lizard will hide in its burrow to stay cool in the hottest part of the day.

A camel can go a week without water. The hump on its back stores fat.

Fennec foxes have very big ears which help them to stay cool.

Grasslands

Grasslands are big areas of land mainly covered with grass. Here are some animals that live on African grasslands.

leopard

giraffe

zebra

hippo

lion

Can you cover each label and name each animal?

The Arctic and Antarctic

The areas at the top and bottom of the Earth are the Arctic and Antarctic. It's always cold and icy, but some animals do survive there.

Arctic

Antarctic

Can you notice something similar about all these animals?

snowy owl

polar bear

Arctic fox

Arctic hare

baby harp seal

Antarctic penguins

There are no penguins in the Arctic, but millions of them live in the Antarctic in huge groups called colonies. Here are five different kinds.

Emperor penguins are the tallest at about 1m (39in).

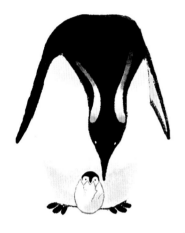

Emperor parents keep their eggs warm on their feet until the eggs hatch.

emperor

Rockhoppers are the smallest at about 50cm (20in).

rockhopper

gentoo

chinstrap

macaroni

The world of people

Most people don't live in forests, deserts or other natural places. They live in towns or cities where there are many things to do and see.

How many of these places do you have in your town?

theatre

fire station

police station

museum

post office

train station

playground

Smallton Hospital

school

hospital

café

library

shop

25

Map of the world

Here's a map of the whole world.
Do you know where you live?.

Can you name all of the
oceans and continents?
Try covering the labels.

Arctic Ocean

Asia

Pacific Ocean

Australia

Indian Ocean

Europe

Africa

Antarctica

North America

Atlantic Ocean

Southern Ocean

South America

North

East

West

South

Our World quiz

Can you answer all these questions about our world?
Look back through the book to help you, if you like.
The answers are on page 32.

1. Which of these things were made by people?

a) volcano   b) factory   c) cave   d) city   e) iceberg

2. Which of these animals might you find living in or near a river?

a) kingfisher   b) salmon   c) octopus   d) camel   e) otter

3. Match each picture to a type of weather.

stormy
foggy
snowy
sunny

a)   b)   c)   d)

Spotting game

Can you find all of these things in the book?

turtle

fire station

jellyfish

farm

macaw

frog

brain coral

shark

Where do they live?

Can you remember where these animals live?
Look back through the book to help you, if you like.

fennec fox

emperor penguin

zebra

ray

All the answers are on page 32.

Glossary

Antarctic – the very cold area at the bottom of the Earth. The Antarctic is a continent.

Arctic – the very cold area at the top of the Earth, covered in ice and snow.

city – an area where lots of people live, with many buildings and roads.

cloud – lots of tiny drops of water all together. Rain falls from clouds.

continent – one of the seven huge areas that the land on Earth is divided into.

coral reef – lots of tiny sea animals joined together.

desert – an area where it rains very little.

equator – an imaginary line that goes around the middle of the Earth.

grasslands – large areas of land that are covered with grass.

hibernation – when animals sleep through the winter.

jungle – another word for a rainforest.

man-made – made by people, for example cities and factories.

migration – when animals move from one area to another.

natural – not made by people, for example deserts and mountains.

ocean – a very large area of sea water.

rainforest – a large, thick forest found in the hot areas of the world around the equator. It rains almost every day in rainforests.

sea – a large area of salt water.

season – one of the four parts that the year is divided into: spring, summer, autumn and winter.

town – an area where lots of people live, with many buildings and roads.

weather – what it is like outside, for example if it is sunny, windy, rainy, and so on.

Index

Answers

p. 7 Man-made or natural? Man-made: hat, book, button, cup. Natural: leaf, stone, feather, shell.

p. 13 River animals: a) otter; b) kingfisher; c) heron; d) frog; e) fish.

p. 17 Kinds of coral: a) sea fan; b) bird's-nest coral; c) bubble coral; d) brain coral.

p. 27 Our world quiz: 1. b, d; 2. a, b, e; 3. a) foggy, b) sunny, c) stormy, d) snowy.

p. 28 Spotting game: turtle p. 14, fire station p. 24, jellyfish p. 15, farm p. 7, macaw p. 19, frog p. 13, brain coral p. 17, shark p. 15.

Where do they live? 1. desert, 2. Antarctic, 3. African grasslands, 4. ocean.

LEONARDO
DA VINCI

with an essay by WALTER PATER

Phaidon

Phaidon Press Limited, 5 Cromwell Place, London SW7

Published in the United States by Phaidon Publishers, Inc
and distributed by Praeger Publishers, Inc
111 Fourth Avenue, New York, N.Y. 10003

This edition first published 1971

ISBN 0 7148 1482 2
Library of Congress Catalog Card Number: 72–141062

Printed in Great Britain
Text printed by Hazell Watson & Viney Limited, Aylesbury
Plates printed at The Curwen Press Limited, London